101 Easy, Wacky, Crazy Activities for Young Children

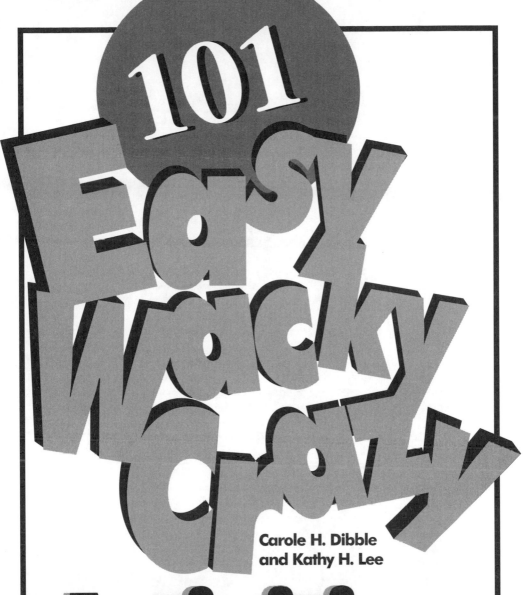

101
Easy
Wacky
Crazy

Carole H. Dibble
and Kathy H. Lee

Activities
For Young Children

gryphon house®, inc.
Beltsville, MD

Gryphon House books are available at special discount when purchased in bulk for special premiums and sales promotions as well as for fund-raising use. Special editions or book excerpts also can be created to specification. For details, contact the Director of Marketing at the address below.

Photographs by Catherine Carr.   Illustrations by K. Whelan Dery.

Library of Congress Cataloging-in-Publication Data
Dibble, Carole H., 1962
101 easy, wacky, crazy activities for young children / Carole H. Dibble and Kathy H. Lee.
    p. cm.
ISBN 0-87659-207-8
1, Creative activities and seat work. 2. Amusements. I. Title: One hundred one easy, wacky, crazy activities for young children. II. Title: Easy, wacky, crazy activities for young children. III. Lee, Kathy H., 1968- IV. Title.

LB1027.25 .D52 1999

00-024516

Table of Contents

We have written this book for "real" adults who are not afraid to let children explore and take charge of their own learning. Exploration encourages children to think creatively, to solve problems, and to discover the joy of learning.

This ideas in this book help young children experience the delight of **doing,** rather than simply looking for a specified outcome or product. The type of activities adults present to children reflect what they believe about children. If adults believe children are incomplete, empty vessels waiting to be filled with knowledge, then success will be measured by the children's ability to repeat what they are taught. We believe that children come to this world as complete beings, ready and capable of constructing knowledge based on experience. This means children learn through daily experiences and discoveries.

Although we have laughed at ourselves and hope to make you laugh, we do take the work of working with children very seriously! We are passionate about improving the quality of care and experiences for young children. The objective of this book is to teach adults about the value of the process of learning and to inspire teachers and parents to try new learning experiences with children.

We invite you to use this book as a journal. Feel free to change these ideas to make them work for you and your children. Personalize this book to help you remember special times with special people.

So-Let's get started!

Getting Started

We wish we could say that we are truly famous and well-respected scholars, but it's not true.

We wish we could say that this book will solve every problem, but it's not true.

We can say we know some famous and well-respected scholars, and we hope they would approve of these ideas: that's true.

We can say we tried to make this a fun and easy-to-use book: that's true.

We can say the process is more important than the product. THAT'S TRUE!

Thank you

We want to thank all the teachers, educators, and children who have inspired these ideas.

Thanks to the staff, parents, and children of Peachtree Presbyterian Child Development Center, Atlanta, Georgia and Little Faces Learning Center, Atlanta, Georgia for allowing us to play and photograph play in their programs.

A special thanks to our families and friends. Without them, this book would not be a reality.

A Place for One

Bring in that big appliance box, bring out the tempera paint, provide some paint rollers, and make that box a home. Add pillows and a soft blanket and this is a great place to relax and get away from it all.

Of course a soft place for escape is only the beginning for this box. With a little help, this box may become a home, a space ship, or even a car. Imagination is an amazing thing.

> *Above all let children know you love them, no matter what.* —Angela Stewart

Just take

Large appliance box
Tempera paint
Paint rollers
Paintbrushes
Pillows
Blankets

This idea was special because...

Accordion

(This idea came from Kathy Evins, a real mom and a real teacher. This is her real idea!)

First, the children cut strips from a paper bag. Next, they fold the strips accordion style. Now, they are ready to paint the strips with tempera paint. After the strips dry, they can glue them to paper or use them with other collage materials to create their own multi-media creation.

Just take

Paper bags
Scissors
Tempera paint
Paintbrushes
Glue
Paper

This would be super to do after reading books by Eric Carle! He uses multi-media to create the artwork for his books.

Write your original ideas here. Mail them to us, and we may include your idea in our next book.

Bag It

This is one of several activities that use resealable plastic bags. In one bag, place a big blob of finger paint. Now seal the bag! Children can draw in the paint, using their fingers or round, dull objects. It's fun to refrigerate the paint-filled bag before painting to add a whole new dimension to this process.

But don't stop there. Try a mixture of shaving cream and food coloring or flour and a few drops of water. Every concoction creates a different texture and feel.

This is a great activity for toddlers. As long as the bag is sealed well it is also a fun activity for the car for preschoolers. They can draw and write without the paper waste.

(This picture has nothing to do with this activity. We just liked the picture.)

Just take

Small plastic resealable bags
Finger paint
Spoon

Next time I will try...

Bubbles Are a Blast

Mix water and dishwashing detergent to create your own bubble solution. Drinking straws make great bubble wands. Just bend the straw in several places and tuck one end of the straw inside the other, creating a circle. If you find yourself without bubble wands, don't fret, make a circle by placing your two hands together, thumb to thumb and pointer to pointer. Presto! It's a human wand. Try placing bubbles in a small swimming pool and use hula hoops as bubble wands (very cool!).

Just take

A deep bowl or dish pan
Dishwashing liquid (we prefer Dawn)
Water

I love bubbles because...

_____

_____

_____

Bath Time

This isn't bath time, although children might look as if they have had a bath after they finish. Create soapy water in a large tub, sink, or sensory table and let children bathe baby dolls. This is a great way to get dolls clean while children have fun. Be sure to have plenty of towels on hand for the wet babies. We mean children and dolls!

Just take

Water

Liquid soap

Large tub or sink

Dolls or other items to bathe

Towels

Offer unbreakable dishes or other toys. Bath time for the pets (stuffed ones!) could be right around the corner.

Great outside activity!

Children wanted to bathe...

Bottles of Stuff

Save soda, sport drink, and water bottles (any clear plastic bottle will do). Fill the bottles with a variety of materials, such as corn syrup, sequins, bells, confetti, little cars, oil, water, colored water, beads, etc. Add floating objects to liquids, such as sequins in corn syrup and beads in colored water, or just put objects to shake or view in a bottle without liquid. Super glue the lid on and you have a variety of new toys.

Just take

Clear plastic bottles
Corn syrup
Confetti
Super glue

These bottles are great for babies and toddlers. Jingle bells (without liquid) add sounds and pretty sequins (with liquid) catch their eye.

Older kids can make their own "lava lamp" in a similar way. Just add food coloring diluted with a little water to create those cool colored bubbles.

When Kathy adopted her son, John Michael, one of the teachers in the school gathered confetti from the baby shower and ribbons from the gifts and made a special bottle for John Michael. This was one of his favorite things to play with as a baby and now he loves to hear the story of his bottle.   —Carole

I made this idea better when...

BOX Blocks

Do you need new blocks for children to play with? Reuse juice boxes by covering with contact paper or painting (add a bit of detergent to the paint so it sticks to the juice box), and build your way to a new tall tower.

(A great way to get lots of blocks without spending any extra money and recycling, too!)

Wiggly Blocks

Here is a neat treat to have while playing with box blocks. Dissolve four packages of flavored gelatin and one package of unflavored gelatin (such as Knox) in four cups of boiling water while stirring. (Only adults pour and stir boiling water.) Chill until firm and cut into shapes.

Just take

Juice boxes (empty, clean, and dry)
Contact paper or paint and
paint brushes

Other great materials for blocks:

Brains?!

Dissolve the gelatin in water. Heat on the stove (adult only) while stirring constantly (not necessarily to boiling, a couple of minutes will do). Pour into two tubs (like whipped topping or large margarine tubs). Chill until firm (the freezer works if you're in a hurry). Dump onto a washable surface and provide children with colored water and pipettes. Soon, you'll see why it is called brains.

Just take

16 packets (4 boxes) plain, unflavored gelatin, such as Knox
11 cups of water
Stove (adult only)
Saucepan (adult only)
Margarine tubs or small bowls for molds
Washable surface or shallow dish
Colored water (see idea #97)
Pipettes (available at most school supply stores)

After children are done playing with it, rinse the gelatin in cold water to rinse out most of the color. Reheat the gelatin. It will melt so you can remold it and play again.

You never can tell when you do an act, what the result will be. —Ella Wheeler

My brain liked...

Bring in the Bugs

That's right! Send children out with small plastic bottles or maybe even a butterfly net. They will come back with living and dead treasures of bugs. Have magnifying glasses on hand for children to check out their "finds" up close. (After a half-hour or so, release the bugs outdoors.)

Big kids may want to create a habitat to keep their new pet. A large jar with holes punched in the lid will work or an aquarium topped with an aluminum screen makes a nice home for bugs. Be sure to provide leaves and plants for a natural habitat. Find out what the bug eats and provide it with appropriate food. Some insects and spiders make interesting pets.

Just take

A plastic jar with a lid
or a butterfly net
Magnifying glass

BAG THAT SEALS

Although some children think this is a great activity, other children are not fond of bugs. Honor children's feelings when planning. John Michael, Kathy's son, does NOT like bugs. On the other hand, Christopher, one of Carole's sons, thinks bugs are great and is the first to spot a bug and get down to check it out more closely. —Kathy and Carole

I was "buggy" when...

_____

_____

_____

_____

Bubble Rap, Do the Bubble Wrap!

Use bubble wrap to make prints. Just brush paint on the bubble wrap and apply to paper for a print as original as this "Rap."

Just take

Bubble wrap
· **Tempera paint**
Paintbrush
Paper

Resist the urge to pop the bubble,
if you pop then you're in trouble.
That bubble wrap has many uses,
we don't want to hear your excuses.

Let the kids paint and print,
this is more than just a hint.
Bubble wrap is not lacking,
it is more than just for packing.

Try popping the bubbles and repeat the process.

Now that we know you better, we feel we can share with you. We sent this rap to a record company. I know you'll find this hard to believe (we did), but they turned us down in an unkind way. We will try not to let this affect our self-esteem, but please... be kind. —Kathy and Carole

My version of the bubble "rap" is...

_____

_____

_____

_____

Build Your Own House

Collect all of those empty cartons and boxes from your favorite foods and household items. Use a hot glue gun to put them together to make a wall, or a room, or an arch, or maybe an entire house. (Just ask children where to put the boxes and glue them into place.) Start gluing them together end to end or side to side and see where it leads you. The possibilities are endless!

(This house makes a great space for one.)

> It is crucial always to respect the home life and daily experiences of those around us. Any time we deliver statements of judgment, others around us may feel judged. It is important to be sensitive and respect everyone's home and family lifestyle. Acceptance breeds self-esteem in children.   —Carole Dibble

Just take

Empty cartons and boxes such as cereal boxes
Hot glue gun (adult only)

Next time I will make it...smaller, bigger, wider, taller?

_____

_____

_____

_____

Clean Paint

We have all been waiting for the perfect paint product that never stains, doesn't drip, and entertains children for hours. We haven't invented that paint, but this paint is pretty close. Let children make finger paint by mixing liquid soap and powdered tempera paint. The soap makes cleanup a breeze. This is the almost-perfect finger paint!

Just take

Powdered tempera paint

Liquid soap

Paper

Cleanup is even easier during the summer months. Let children run through the sprinkler or just "hose 'em" down.

Funny, but true story

One morning Kathy walked by a toddler room. There stood Hayes in her diaper, painting herself red. Kathy asked, "Hayes, what are you doing?" Hayes replied, "Painting myself red." Because Hayes had touched red paint and experienced it, Hayes understood the color red. I hope she was using clean paint. Dare to be bold!

What I liked best about this idea was...

_____

_____

_____

_____

Construction Sites on the Move

Bring those blocks outside for building with a whole new perspective. When children build with blocks inside, they are generally building on a flat, smooth surface. The ground outside gives construction workers a whole new set of opportunities and challenges. Now, don't worry! The blocks will not get that dirty! Children can wash them in a tub of water on their way back in.

Big kids will love to take their Legos and other small building stuff. They can build cars, and other moving things. They will probably bury some of the parts too. You might suggest they draw maps to chart their block burials.

Just take

The great outdoors

Blocks and other building materials

Tub of soapy water

I got moving when...

_____

_____

_____

_____

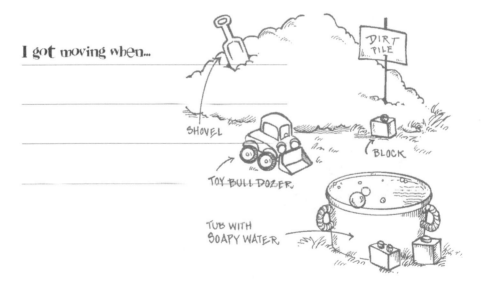

DIRT PILE

SHOVEL

BLOCK

TOY BULL DOZER

TUB WITH SOAPY WATER

Cook Up Some Fun

CLEAN HANDS

Children love to help out in the kitchen, but can we turn the cooking over to the children? Sure we can! They can use cutting boards and plastic knives to create a fruit salad extraordinare. Children can make their own soup, create their own pizzas, or shake up a milkshake (with adult help and supervision when using appliances and hot or sharp tools).

Just take

Cutting board
Plastic knives, forks, and spoons
Food for cutting and cooking
Clean hands
Empty tummies

With older kids, encourage them to plan a menu and take them shopping for the ingredients. Supervise children as they prepare the meal and enjoy the meal they serve. What great skills they are learning! You might be encouraging a future chef, the next famous food critic, or a future parent who makes the best pancakes in the whole world!

CUTTING BOARD

What new recipes did children create?

_____

_____

WATERMELON
BANANA
APPLE
ORANGE
GRAPES

Corporate Elongated Strips of Paper (AKA shredded paper)

Offer to take the shredded paper from offices or businesses. Put out lots (the more the better) of shredded paper and let children play in it, throw it, hide under it, or do anything else fun! When the play is over, save a little for a collage project.

Big kids will have fun experimenting with the shredded paper too. We are sure they will love putting the paper in a large tub and adding water (ooh!). Encourage them to make paintbrushes with paper and tape. Painting with a shredded paper paintbrush is so much fun (and very cheap).

Just take

Shredded paper

Space for children to explore

What did you add to it?

Coverings for Your Head

Kids love to put things on their heads! Provide lots of different hats or even a bucket or two and watch children become a cowboy, a construction worker, a bride, or maybe an alien. You might have a special hat day and wear favorite hats all day long. Don't limit yourself to the traditional hats, any funny hat will do.

Just take Hats

For toddlers make sure there is a mirror nearby. It makes everybody laugh to look at themselves in a hat.

Big kids could take this a step further and make their own hat with newspaper and masking tape. Simply spread out 5-6 sheets of newspaper over your head. Then ask a friend to tape the newspaper around the perimeter of your head to create the base of the brim. Use tape to help form a crown at the top of your head out of the newspaper. Roll up the edges of the newspaper to make the brim of the hat. Paint and decorate, and you are ready to set a new trend in headwear. (If you like this idea, try idea #90.)

More great hat ideas:

Cube Color

Start out with sugar cubes. Provide children with colored water made from food coloring and eyedroppers or pipettes. Children will do the rest. They may stack and color the sugar cubes. Or they may just color them. No matter how children do it, discoveries are on the horizon.

For bigger kids, challenge them to figure out what colors mix to create green, orange, and purple. Another challenge for the older set is to set up experiments estimating how long it will take the color to flow through three stacks of sugar cubes and then observe the process and determine the results. Oh wow! This science and math is fun!

Just take

Sugar cubes
Colored water
Eyedroppers or pipettes

Use these cubes to make colored lemonade or crush them to decorate a birthday cake!

There is nothing like a group of four-year-olds to bring one down to normal size. —Docia Zavitikovsky

The great thing about this idea is...

Do Windows!

We do not believe in child labor, but we do believe in child fun! Provide children with windows (any windows they can reach will do), a bucket of water, a sponge, and a squeegee.

Just take

Buckets
Water
Sponges and
squeegees
Windows

Put it all together and you have window washing at its finest, while having a blast! This is a super summer day experience.

Little ones will enjoy squirting the windows with water in a squirt bottle. Bigger kids will enjoy actually "doing windows" with cleaning solution.

What happened when you tried this idea?

Don't Throw Those Markers Away

I know you think dried-out markers are ready to throw away, but don't be too hasty. All children need is paper, cups of water, and dried-out markers. Now they are ready to draw. They just dip the tip of the marker in the water and they're ready to do a lovely watercolor drawing.

Do the older kids want an additional challenge? Provide them with watercolor paper, cups of water, paintbrushes, and old markers. They use the brushes to spread water on the paper, then color over the water with the markers to create a watercolor masterpiece.

Shhh! Don't share this idea too quickly. Just offer to take old markers from anyone who will give them to you.

Just take

Paper
Cups of water
Dried-out washable
or watercolor
markers

CUP OF WATER

Children enjoyed...

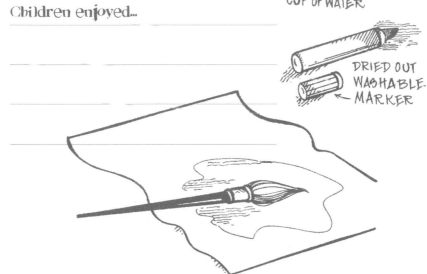

DRIED OUT
WASHABLE
MARKER

Dough Dough

This is the dough recipe you know exists, but can't ever find when you need it. Combine 2 cups of flour, 1 cup of salt, 2 cups of water, 1 tablespoon of oil, and 4 teaspoons of cream of tartar. Microwave or heat on high, stirring after each minute until it is the correct consistency. In our humble opinion this is the best dough around!

Just take

Flour
Salt
Water
Oil
Cream of tartar
Measuring cups and spoons
Mixing spoon and bowl
Microwave or stove

Little kids can play with this playdough because it is made of nontoxic ingredients.

Kathy says it's great to use old cookie cutters with this dough. Carole suggests that you cut one-inch thick dowels about six inches long to use as rolling pins. (Kids can sand the ends before using them for rolling).
—Kathy and Carole

I liked the authors' suggestions because...

_____

_____

_____

_____

Dress Me Up

Pack up the dress-up clothes for the day. Bring out leftover fabric, sheets, tablecloths, and sashes. Children will tailor clothes to their own taste as they drape, wrap, and tie themselves. These designers will be ready to show their wares at your next local fashion show.

Who knows? You may want them to design your next party attire! Hey, that's a good idea! Encourage bigger kids to design an outfit for themselves or someone else. Find a seamstress and have it made.

Just take

Fabric

Mirror

Kids (and adults) ready for a makeover

I was glad to see...

CAPE

DRAGON

Dyeing Eggs in September!

Children LOVE dyeing eggs. It doesn't seem fair that children only get to dye eggs in the springtime. Dare to be different! Let children dye eggs throughout the year. Have an egg hunt. Read the nursery rhyme of "Humpty Dumpty," and let children make their own Humpty Dumptys out of hard-boiled eggs.

Just take

Hard-boiled eggs
Food coloring
Vinegar
Water

FOOD COLORING

After the egg hunt, you are ready to make egg salad. Let children peel the eggs themselves. (You may want to rinse the eggs afterwards to make sure the egg salad isn't crunchy.) Children add a little mayonnaise, mustard, pickles, or whatever you find pleasing to the palate. Stir and yum! You're ready to eat.

You can use a raw egg to tell the story of "Humpty Dumpty," but remember that raw eggs can carry bacteria. Be sure to clean it up, and don't let children play with raw eggs.

What surprised me was...

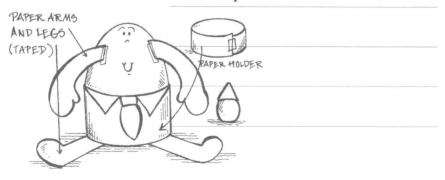

PAPER ARMS AND LEGS (TAPED)

PAPER HOLDER

Ease that Easel on Outside

Drag that easel outside. Provide plenty of paint, lots of paper and see what children use for a paintbrush. It may be a pinecone, a leaf, or even their fingers. You might want to have paintbrushes handy, just in case.

No easel? No problem! Just take a sheet or large pieces of paper and hang them on the fence or tape it to a wall. You can even put the paper on the ground and hold it down with sticks or rocks. The uneven surface will add a new dimension to the art.

Just take

The real outdoors
Easel, fence, wall, or rocks
Paint
Paper
Imagination
Paintbrushes, optional

I eased into this activity because...

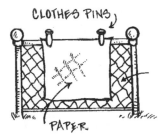

CLOTHES PINS

PAPER

(PLACE OVER ROOTS AND RUN PASTEL STICK OVER ROOTS)

TREE

ROOTS

PAPER

Field Trips to You

There are so many obstacles to field trips so it makes sense to bring the field trip to you. Great field trips to bring to you are the plumber, the landscapers, the dog groomer, and others who have professions that are interesting to children. Or take advantage of "instant" field trips by asking the plumber who came to fix the clogged line if children can watch while the work is done. Next time a tree is cut in your neighborhood take the time to stop and watch. It truly is a learning experience.

Just take

A telephone book!

Beauty, in its truest form, is seeing the world through my child's eyes: seeing the excitement, the wonder, and the innocence. When I allow myself to do that, I am my happiest.   —Laurie Numedahl-Meuwissen

Children say the most amazing things.

_____

_____

_____

Floaties

It is time to pull out those bags again. Add water, sequins, confetti, and other floatable fun stuff. Seal carefully! This is a no mess activity, unless the bag comes unsealed, and then you can call this a water activity! Hint: Don't use anything that has sharp edges; it will break the bag. And don't overfill the bag.

For more fun, substitute baby oil for water. You can freeze the bag and observe what happens over time. Wait a minute, this just became science!

Those who know how to play can easily leap over the adversities of life. —Iglulik Proverb

This combination worked best...

Just take

Resealable
plastic bags
Water
Sequins or confetti
Small items like
buttons or sequins

Fly Guts

In a large tub or bowl, mix together shavings of Ivory soap, shredded toilet paper, and water. Don't use just one bar of soap and a few sheets of toilet paper, go wild! This is an activity where more is better.

Just take

Large tub or bowl
Bar soap, such as Ivory
Cheese grater
Toilet paper
Water

People always ask us what to do with the fly guts after they make it. We say, use your imagination. Some people use it to make snowballs, others add food coloring so it looks more like real guts, and others bury treasure in it.

What happened?

_____

_____

_____

_____

Fly Paper
(Not to be confused with Fly Guts, idea #26)

Tape up a big sheet of butcher paper, and spray on the 3M Super 77 Adhesive. See what children will "catch" on this sticky paper. They can add collage items, the ever-popular tissue paper, family pictures, nature items, or anything else. They will likely be more creative than we could ever be.

(The 3M Super 77 spray has a strong odor. Be sure to spray the paper when children are not in the room and air the room out before they return.)

This activity is great for little kids who love to take things off, put things on, take things off, put things on. You get the idea.

Just take

Paper (large sheets of butcher paper work great)

Tape

3M Super 77 adhesive spray (adults only in a well-ventilated area)

Collage materials

I knew I was stuck when...

Fort Building

You don't have to be a master builder to have fun creating a fort. It only takes wood, nails, hammers, and safety gear. Many home goods stores have wood scraps they will donate, and you provide the rest. Let children plan and create their own forts. They will have fun putting the wood together and building it themselves.

Just take

Wood
Hammers
Nails
Safety goggles

This activity could turn into a major project for big kids. They could visit an architect, getting tips for their fort. They could design and build their very own space. How cool is that!

Wait, don't forget the younger ones. Using Styrofoam and golf tees (larger ones are better) toddlers can use a plastic hammer and pound away. Safety tip: Saw off the tips of the golf tees to keep things safe.

I knew I was up a tree when...

HAMMER

WOOD

SAFTEY GOGGLES

NAILS

Framed Fabric

Do you have any picture frames that don't fit in with your new décor? Donate these frames (just the frames, no glass) to children's creativity. Start with fabric (any fabric will do). Cut the fabric into strips or shapes. Take out a shallow bowl and pour in some good ole' school glue. Water down the glue until it becomes sort of milky. Dip the fabric into the glue and paste it on the old or out-of-date picture frame. Cover the entire frame with fabric. Let the creation dry, and, just like that, you have a new frame.

Although these make great gifts, one way to make them even better is to put a picture of the frame creator in it.

Just take

Used picture frame
Fabric
Scissors
Glue
Bowl
Water

This activity worked well because...

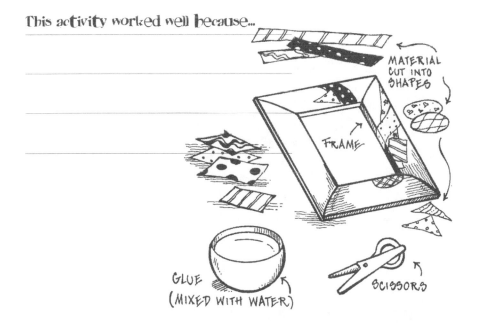

MATERIAL CUT INTO SHAPES

FRAME

GLUE (MIXED WITH WATER)

SCISSORS

Glarch, Gak, or Whatever It Is Called

In a container, stir together glue and liquid starch. Add some more starch or glue, stir some more. Continue this process until you have a putty-like consistency. You can refrigerate it, add color to it, or just play with it the way it is. Oh, and don't forget to name it.

Just take

A cup or bowl
Glue
Liquid starch
Mixing spoon

The fascinating thing about this mixture is it changes. The more you play with it, the more rubbery it gets. It will even bounce. One time we added a little shaving cream and it was so cool. I wonder what you will think of to do with this.

(Kathy says, "If it's stringy, you need more glue and if it's sticky, you need more starch." She calls it glarch.)

Now I know what you mean by messy.

Hose 'Em Down

This seems so simple, you are going to wish you had thought to write it down and become rich and famous like us. Just pull out that water hose and have a good time. Spray 'em, squirt 'em, and be prepared to get wet and have fun yourself!

Bigger kids can have fun making sprinklers for little kids. They may even try out their handiwork and run through the sprinkler themselves once or twice.

Just take

Water hose
Warm, sunny day

I will try this activity again because...

GOGGLES

HOSE

HOT Plate

Stop by the local home goods store and ask for leftover tiles. Offer the tiles to children as a canvas for their art. Children can paint or print on the tile. Once the tile is dry, shellac (only adults use the shellac) the masterpiece and you have a super gift for that someone special.

Just take

Floor or wall tiles
Paint
Paintbrushes or other painting utensils
Shellac (adults only in a well-ventilated area)
Someone special to give the hot plate to

Wouldn't it be wonderful to put a child's handprint on a tile each year of their childhood? Frame the tiles as a memory, or if you are really handy, make them into a tabletop. What a great present to give back to a child!

If we allow children to show us what they can do rather than merely accepting what they normally do, I feel certain we would be in for some grand surprises.
—Mem Fox

I enjoyed observing...

Ice Sculpture

Freeze water in small buckets, large bowls, or old milk jugs with the tops cut off. After the water freezes, dump the ice into a big tub. Encourage children to create an ice sculpture using warm water in pitchers or eyedroppers. Melt your way to a new creation. Add food coloring or colored water to make it more interesting.

Simply place several blocks of ice in a bowl and let the younger kids add water. Watching the ice melt is breathtaking enjoyment for this age group.

Imagination is the highest kite one can fly.
—Lauren Bacall

What meltdowns occurred?

Just take

Small buckets, large bowls, or milk jugs
Water
Freezer
Large tub
Pitchers, pipettes, cups, or eyedroppers
Food coloring or colored water, optional

If the Shoe Fits

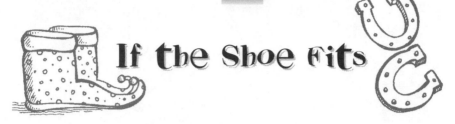

Take dress-up to a whole new level by allowing children to try on each other's shoes. Mix in other shoes (clown shoes, baby shoes, horseshoes, etc.) for children to try on. Make sure you let them try your shoes on, too. Ask children if they think their shoes will fit like their friends' shoes. They will have fun comparing and contrasting their shoes to their friends' shoes.

Just take

Shoes
Feet

It might be fun to make a chart that shows which shoe is the biggest and which shoe is the smallest.

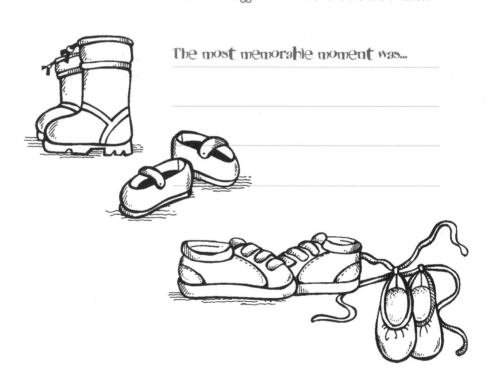

The most memorable moment was...

It's a Wrap

After big gift-giving events, children can use leftover rolls of wrapping paper. Children always want to help wrap presents, so let them! Bring out rolls of old wrapping paper, scissors, boxes, and bows, and don't forget the tape. The great news is—no one has to wait for the special event to open a present.

Let children choose toys or objects to wrap and then a box isn't necessary. These "gifts" are special for parents, friends, and other important folks, and the pride shows on the face of the giver when the present is opened.

Just take

Rolls of wrapping paper
Boxes
Bows
Tape
Scissors

I improved this idea by...

It's Tool Time

Kids love to put on a tool belt. I don't know why, I just know it's true. Some large home improvement stores sell child-size tool belts or aprons, but you can make your own with a strip of fabric for the belt and something to create loops for hanging tools. Now your handy helpers are ready to help.

Just take

A tool belt or apron
Child-size tools

It is great to let little helpers put on their tool belts when you get your tools out. Children are less likely to touch a dangerous tool if they have safe tools of their own that they are allowed to use.

My best tools are...

_____

_____

_____

Jump for Joy! It's Junk!

Oh, the treasures to be found at the junkyard! Have you ever thought about an old tub as a great place for reading books? What could children do with a few spare car parts like hubcaps or a steering wheel? The junkyard is a field of dreams (and good stuff) for a resourceful person.

You don't even have to go to the junkyard to find "junk." Sometimes our homes seem to collect lots of stuff that we will never use again. Why not pull out the clothes, linens, and household equipment that you have stored away. Come on, you are never going to wear that bridesmaid's dress again.

Take bigger kids on a field trip to the junkyard to collect their own goodies. Be careful, they might want to bring home the junkyard dog.

I jumped for joy when...

_____

_____

_____

Just take

Junk

MITTENS

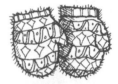

BIKE TIRE

TEAPOT

TENNIS RACKET

LOCK

HALLOWEEN MASK

BASKET

Kitchen Gadgets

What can you do with all the stuff in your third-from-the-left kitchen drawer? You know, the one with I-might-need-this-one-day kitchen gadgets, like the sifter and the egg yolk separator. We have a solution for you. Get those gadgets out and let children start painting with them. This idea is so much fun you might have to give up some of the gadgets that you actually use.

Just for fun, create a painting (on one sheet of paper) using one gadget and one color of paint per day. Layer the paint and discover a whole new meaning to process art.

Just take

A kitchen drawer full of unused gadgets

Paint

Paper

A chef's hat might be fun

The most interesting gadget used was...

Let the Sun Shine on Your Shoulders

Head 'em up and move 'em out doors. Take those sketchpads (or paper attached to cardboard or a clipboard) outside with colored pencils. The colors, smells, and sounds of the big outdoors will surely inspire children as they draw and write on their pads. The colors of the different seasons may also inspire budding artists.

The most important thing, however, is to go outside and take the time to take in the sights, smell, and sounds. Then give children the opportunity to record what they see and feel through drawing.

Just take

Sketchpads or paper and cardboard

Colored pencils or crayons

My face was shining when...

Let's Go Camping

Bring a tent out of the wilderness to the inside. The ideas are endless. It makes a great "place for one" or a fun place to have lunch. A child might climb in with a book or maybe a bunch of books.

Just take

A tent, or a large blanket or sheet and rope

Younger kids will have fun just climbing in and out of the tent. Bigger kids might have fun "roasting" marshmallows and making smores by the "fireplace" or on the "grill." Some kids will probably insist on sleeping in the tent. I say, OKAY!

Watch out! If someone is missing, they might be napping in the tent!

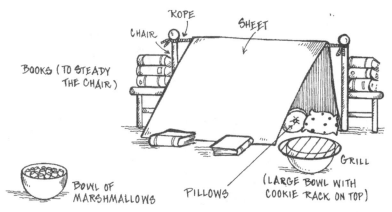

ROPE
CHAIR
SHEET
BOOKS (TO STEADY THE CHAIR)
GRILL
(LARGE BOWL WITH COOKIE RACK ON TOP)
BOWL OF MARSHMALLOWS
PILLOWS

I camped out on this idea because...

Let's Go Swimming

It begins with a kiddie pool. It continues with lots of packing material (the recyclable kind that melts). It gets really wild with water. The packing material melts and gets really gooey. Be prepared with swimsuits, soap, and a hose for cleanup.

Children don't have to swim in this creation to enjoy it. This activity is lots of fun in a large tub, squishing it with hands.

What did you think? What did you really think?

Just take

Swimming pool (the small plastic ones)
Packing material (the kind made from corn-starch)
Water

PACKING MATERIAL IN WATER

HOSE

POOL

Magic Feathers

Put out a tub of feathers and a large turkey baster (or a small plastic baster with the end cut off). Children squeeze the turkey baster and release. Magically, feathers disappear. Children love to make things "disappear." As they release the baster the feathers are drawn into the baster. They can count the feathers or just wonder at how this magic works. Wow!

Just take

A dish pan or tub
Feathers (just a few small ones)
A large turkey baster

Talk with children, letting them explain to you how the "magic" works. If they don't really understand the displacement of air, that is okay. When a child develops a theory on how something happens they are learning to be explorers in the future.

(Be on the lookout! We hear this is how several professional magicians got their start.)

I was light as a feather when...

FEATHERS

TUB

TURKEY BASTER

Making Tracks

Start with a play car. Dip the wheels in paint, and Make Tracks on paper. Children can use different cars and colors, comparing the tracks or having tracks run in many directions. They can match the color of the car to the paint for a matching experience. This is a great activity to help young children build vocabulary as children describe the cars and the tracks.

Just take

Play cars
Paint
Paper

After making tracks with paint, head to the sandbox with the cars and trucks and make tracks in damp sand. Talk about how the tracks are similar and how they are different.

I knew I was on the "fast track" when...

_____

_____

_____

_____

Many Marbles or Is It Mini Marbles?

Put a piece of paper (any paper) in a box (any box). Next add drops of paint (any paint, any color). Finally, add marbles (many marbles or mini marbles). The more marbles, the more fun! Roll 'em around and bounce 'em up and down! Now this is art!

Just take

Paper
Box with a lid
Tempera paint
Marbles (or golf balls)

For the little ones try golf balls instead of marbles. Golf balls don't pose a choking hazard and they work just as well.

I "boxed" up laughing when...

_____

_____

_____

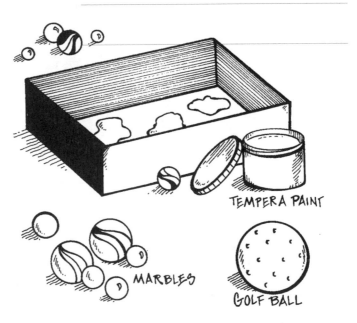

TEMPERA PAINT

MARBLES

GOLF BALL

Memories

So what do you do with all those pictures you take during the year? What about the menu from a restaurant or the tickets from the puppet show? What do you do with all this stuff? Make a memory wall! Devote a wall or area to memories. Display pictures and keepsakes from events throughout the year. Don't forget the everyday events!

Just take

Photographs

Keepsakes

Older kids may arrange groups of pictures on colored paper and use stickers and paper designs to make the display interesting. It is always fun to add "cartoon bubbles" to create talking pictures.

Traditions are the coat racks on which you hang your memories.
       —Carolyn James

My best memory of this idea is...

Mississippi Mud

(We both grew up in Mississippi so we named this
activity in honor of our home state.)
(Catherine Carr, the photographer for this book,
is also from Mississippi)

If you have been digging in the dirt lately, you may have noticed that not all dirt is created equal. It comes in all sorts of shades and colors. Let children mix water with different shades of dirt to create different shades of "paint." Then create a really earthy picture.

Just take

**Dirt in various shades
of brown, red, and
gray
Water
Paper
Paintbrushes or hands**

Facts about Mississippi
- Capital City: Jackson
- State Flower: Magnolia
- State Bird: Cardinal
- Elvis Presley was born in Tupelo and so was Carole.
- Kathy thinks Mississippi State is the greatest school!

What I liked about this idea is...

Mystery Box

Children love it when you show them something new. With a mystery box, this is easy to do. Use a decorative box and fill it with different items. Some suggestions include pinecones of all shapes and sizes, an assortment of buttons or zippers, or things that are red. Gather items and let children guess the theme.

How does the box get decorated? You can decorate it or give the kids colorful pieces of contact paper to peel and stick and create a truly enticing mystery box.

Older kids love to create their own games. Ask children to figure out how many ways they can sort the items in the box. Or ask a group of children to select the items for the box and create with their own Mystery Box game.

Just take

A deep box with a lid
Bright contact paper
Items with a common theme

(ROUND ITEMS)

BEAD

NICKEL

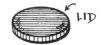
LID

BALL OF YARN

I'm thinking out of the box now because...

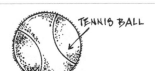
TENNIS BALL

DECORATED BOX

Oil and Water Don't Mix

This one is such an old idea it was around even before you were born. The truth is, times have changed, but this fact remains the same. Put out a pan with water. Have the oil ready to add. Children are always amazed that it just won't mix. Let them add a little food coloring to really shake things up.

Just take

A pan or bowl
Water
Oil
Spoon
Food coloring,
optional

Let bigger kids guess what will happen before they mix oil and water. (Yes, this is known as a hypothesis.) Then provide them with other elixirs to mix just to see what happens when they meet.

Laughter is the shortest distance between two people.
    —Victor Borge

It shook things up when...

Ooey Gooey

Put cornstarch in a large tub or sensory table. Let children play in the dry cornstarch, experiencing the texture and consistency. Next, let children add water to the cornstarch. Encourage children to describe what happens. Talk about the change in the texture and consistency. Notice, it feels firm to pick up and then seems to melt in your hands (unlike M&M's).

Try adding dry tempera to the cornstarch or liquid tempera to the cornstarch and water.

Just take

Cornstarch
Water
Plastic tub or sensory table

This mixture feels like...

_____

_____

_____

_____

Paint the Town

House painters get to use great painting equipment. Don't let them have all the fun! Just put out paint rollers and paint trays and you're ready to paint the town. (No paint necessary). At the end of this activity cleanup is a breeze.

Just take

Paint rollers (they come in all sizes)
Paint trays
Paint, optional

Bigger kids might enjoy helping you paint shelves or other furniture (with paint). This could be a group project. Make sure you are supervising or you could end up with walls that are lavender with polka dots.

How long did it take before someone asked for paint?

_____

_____

_____

Paper Collage Minus the Paper

Put out the collage materials, but no paper. These collages are paper free and 3-D. This idea takes collage-making to a new dimension. Children create sculptures, not just pictures.

For the young ones, go ahead and give them some paper. Put the glue on the paper for the very young. Offer a small variety of materials. As their fine motor skills develop they can graduate to collages without paper.

We must do the things we think we cannot do..
—Eleanor Roosevelt

It was crazy, but children liked...

_____

_____

_____

_____

Just take

A variety of collage materials such as
Popsicle sticks
Sequins
Buttons
Small pieces of tissue paper
Small pieces of construction paper
Drinking straws
Small pieces of colored plastic
Small wood shapes
Aluminum foil wrap
Styrofoam trays
Googly eyes
Pipe cleaners
Glue, paste, tape

Piece It Together

Give children a piece of cardboard cut in the shape of a picture frame. Provide them with jigsaw puzzle pieces (the 445 pieces you can find of the 500 piece puzzle) and glue. Let children paste the puzzle pieces onto the cardboard. They can glue on as many pieces as they want. After the glue dries, children can paint the frame. Now it's ready for the perfect picture!

Just take

Cardboard frames
Puzzle pieces
Glue
Paint
Paintbrushes

If you're not into picture frames, but you still have 445 pieces from the 500-piece puzzle, just leave out the cardboard frame. Children will enjoy creating three-dimensional sculptures using glue and the puzzle pieces.

Big kids can use puzzle pieces to create mosaic-like pictures. Instead of colored tiles, they use colored puzzle pieces to create a picture of many small parts that makes an interesting whole.

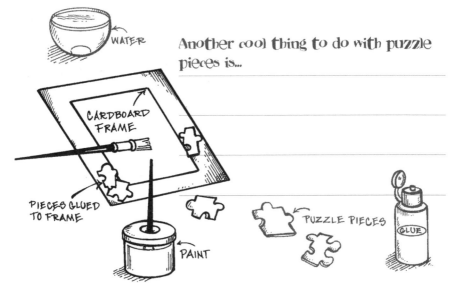

Another cool thing to do with puzzle pieces is...

WATER

CARDBOARD FRAME

PIECES GLUED TO FRAME

PAINT

PUZZLE PIECES

GLUE

Planting the Day Away

Planting seeds is an excellent way to help children discover living things. The choice of seeds is endless. This process can be as simple as planting a few seeds in a cup and watching them grow in your window. If children are interested, grow an actual garden outside. Either way, children will enjoy watching their gardens grow.

Sunflower, daisy, and grass seeds are always favorites for growing. Kids can paint the flowerpots and give the plants away for gifts. Don't forget the little ones with this one. They can help water the plants.

Just take

Potting soil
Pots, cups, or planting areas
Seeds
A green thumb is helpful but not required

What happened to the plants?

_____

_____

_____

_____

Play in the Dirt, Again and Again and Again!

When was the last time you baked up a delicious mud pie? Why not pull out those pie pans, go to your favorite dirt pile, and bake up super fun. Add a little water, lots of time to play, a warm day, and imagination. You're sure to make culinary history!

Just take

Dirt
Pie pans
Spoons or shovels

Even the youngest child will enjoy squishing mud through his or her fingers.

Bigger kids might enjoy making a real pie they can eat after they have created clay cuisine. The following is a pie they can make themselves with very little adult help.

Lemonade Pie

Mix one can defrosted frozen lemonade with one can of sweetened condensed milk. Then stir in one container of thawed whipped topping. Stir with a spoon until all ingredients are blended. It will be pretty fluffy, yellow stuff. Pour the yellow stuff into a prepared graham cracker crumb crust. Chill for a while and you have made yourself a pie.

I won't get bogged down because...

_____

_____

_____

_____

Please Pass the Fish Sticks

Place meals and snacks in containers that allow children to serve themselves in a relaxed environment. Sure, they may get peas on the table, potatoes in their hair, and spill their milk in the beginning, but they will get better. Remember, it's the process not the product, and patience is a virtue. You will be surprised how quickly they will catch on.

Free tip: Use different spoons (maybe a different color or size) for serving. This helps kids remember that they eat with the silver spoons, not the red ones.

I can't pass on this idea because...

_____

_____

_____

Just take

Child-size bowls (for food)
Child-size pitchers for milk (or other drink)
Serving spoons (spoons with color work great)
Food and drink

CHICKEN NUGGETS

SLICED BANANAS

SMALL PITCHER OF MILK

PEAS

SERVING SPOON

APPLESAUCE

CHAIR

Plungers Aren't Just for the Potty Anymore!

Plungers come in many sizes. Let children paint by dipping new plungers into tempera paint and stamping the shapes on paper. The more choices of paint and the more choices of paper, the more individual the art will be. Plunge on!

Just take

Plungers (new ones)
Tempera paint
Paper

Younger kids will enjoy taking the plungers outside with a pail of water and plunging the sidewalk and the windows. You better watch out, they might enjoy plunging you.

Life isn't a matter of milestones-but of moments.
—Rose Kennedy

What did you "plunge" into?

Popsicle Art

Freeze tempera paint in ice cube trays. After 15 minutes, insert popsicle sticks. Continue to freeze until solid. Let children paint with these frozen treats. The more it melts, the more paint is applied.

(These popsicles are for art processes only. They are not currently recognized by the USDA as a significant source of nutrition. They don't taste good, either.)

If children liked this idea, try painting with ice cubes and powdered tempera paint.

All art takes courage.   —Ann Tucker

Just take

Ice cube trays
Tempera paint
Popsicle sticks
Paper

I loved (or loathed) this activity because...

_____

_____

_____

_____

Prop It Up

It starts with long tubes. Where do you get those? See idea #63. Now give them to children and just let their imaginations soar. Challenge children to use the tubes as props and think of all of the things the tubes can be. (Yes, they may be swords.) Props are a great way to get imaginations in high gear and can prompt some interesting stories.

Just take

Long cardboard tubes (wrapping paper tubes or mailing tubes)

Imagination

You don't have to stop with tubes. Next time try paper plates or some other common household items and let children use them as props. Carole's son sees string as spaghetti and a bowl as a boat. It is amazing what imagination can do!

The social life of a child starts when she is born.
—Susanna Millar

I couldn't believe it when...

Pull Out the Potting Soil

Pour a bag of potting soil into a large tub or sensory table. Add cups, spoons, and shovels and you have a great digging area. You can even offer pumpkin seeds or other large seeds to bury in the soil. This is a super sensory activity. If you want to be really daring, add water!

For a change, hide plastic bugs and worms in the soil for the children to discover.

The purpose of play is to go out and be happy...
to lay down cares and have fun for a while.
    —William Dorn

Remember when _____ happened?

Just take

Potting soil
Large tub or sensory table
Cups, spoons, and shovels
Fun stuff to bury
Water

Put a Pencil to It

Bring out a basket of paper, crayons, and pencils and see how children decide to use it. They may think of many reasons to "write." Don't think toddlers are too young for this idea. They will "write" just like they see adults write. Just give them the opportunity and they will find a reason and a way to write.

Just take

Basket
Paper
Pencils
Crayons

One morning Carole was observing in a classroom, using a clipboard and pen. Sarah, a three-year-old, approached Carole and wanted to know what she was doing. Carole said, "I'm watching you play." Sarah said she wanted to watch too. She went to the writing center and got paper and pencil. The teacher noticed and got Sarah a clipboard too. Sarah sat just like Carole and "wrote" about kids playing. This was a wonderful pre-writing moment.

I put a pencil to it when...

Rain, Rain, Don't Go Away!

This is the perfect rainy day activity. Is there a rule that says children may NOT go outside in the rain? We say throw convention aside and head for the outdoors, even in the rain (but not the thunder and lightning). Let children sprinkle powdered tempera paint on paper. Then put on those raincoats and galoshes (boots) and head outside for the perfect water to complete the picture. Let the raindrops do all the work.

This fun way to paint is a natural way to introduce children to people that work outside in the rain. Invite a utility worker to come talk about his or her work and show the tools he or she uses, or maybe talk about why it is important for some people to work in the rain.

Just take

Rain (gentle rain is best)
Powdered tempera
Paper

This idea wasn't a wash because...

_____

_____

_____

_____

Rainbow Flour

Start with those handy dandy spray bottles and a tray of flour (any white flour). Fill the spray bottles with various shades of colored water (see idea #96). Encourage children to squirt the colored water on the tray of flour (instead of you) to experience the change that takes place when water and flour collide.

Just take

Spray bottles
Colored water
Flour
A shallow pan

Okay, so this was fun. Now try other substances from the kitchen and see how a spray of colored water makes them beautiful.

Do you remember the first time you spotted a rainbow? What memories does this bring back for you? Take the time to share these memories with children and help them create their own rainbow memories.

I really liked this idea because...

Reuse It

We aren't talking basic recycling here! We don't mean just toilet paper rolls. We are talking serious reusing and recycling. Contact large industries in your area and ask for their leftovers and discards. Also businesses that sell bulk items, such as home improvement warehouses, often have scrap materials and discards they are happy to share with a teacher or parent. You'll be amazed at the things you'll find, like Plexiglass, labels, and newsprint rolls from the local newspaper. Once we even got a trap door from a bus!

Just take

The yellow pages (yes, we mean the phone directory)

After you gather these materials, be creative. Can the item be used in art projects or as part of a collage? Can children build with it? Can it be written on or painted? And if you are not sure what to do with a treasure you find, ask kids. They always have ideas. Better yet, ask them first. Then see if you can come up with any ideas they didn't.

There is a use for almost anything. —George Washington Carver

What was your greatest find and how did you use it? (Just as important— what was the phone number so you can call to get it again?)

Rock 'n' Roll

Put on your walking shoes and head outside to fill those pockets with rocks. Empty the rocks into a shoebox. Add a little bit of paint and slice of paper. Place the lid on the shoebox, turn on Chuck Berry, and rock 'n' roll.

Children will enjoy shaking their boxes to the rhythm of the music. Take the lid off and discover what a little Rock 'n' Roll can do for you.

Just take

Rocks
Shoebox with a lid
Paper
Paint
Rock 'n' Roll music

This is a great activity for toddlers, school-age kids, and every age in between. With younger children, help them put the paper and paint in the box. They will have no trouble dumping their treasures into the box. Older kids can try other objects and see how it changes the picture.

Did you dance to Chuck Berry? Tell the truth!

Rover, Bring Me That Toy I'm Painting

What a way to add variety to art experiences! Pet toys offer many different shapes, sizes, and textures for children to experience. Dog bones are also fun for children to paint with. Your local dollar store is a good place to stock up on pet supplies for just a few bucks.

Neither of us has a dog named Rover. Carole has a cat named Sassy and a dog named Kirby who used to live with Kathy. Now Kathy has a turtle named Brett Favre (her son named him).

Just take

Pet toys
Paper
Paint

This idea is not for the dogs (or maybe it is for the dogs) because...

See Spot Run

How many times has a child blobbed on a glob of paint where it wasn't supposed to go? The next time this happens, take advantage of the moment. Encourage the child to hold up the blobbed artwork and let the globs run. You should, very quickly, put a piece of paper under the running paint. This is two-for-one art!

Just take

A surprise blob of
paint

Paper

The possible's slow fuse is lit by imagination.
—Emily Dickinson

I couldn't believe it when I spotted...

_____

_____

_____

Self-Portrait

Provide children with a full-length mirror so they can see themselves from head to toe. Supply paint and brushes and let children create their self-portrait directly on the mirror. They may want to paint their whole body or they may want to add features to their reflections. When they have finished painting, have a spray bottle ready for the little artists to clean the mirror for the next child.

Bigger kids can sit across from each other and draw portraits of each other.

These portraits are usually very honest.

Just take

Full-length mirror
Tempera paint
Paintbrushes
Spray bottle
Water
Paper towels or old towels for clean-up

I reflected upon...

Shake, Shake, Shake

Making music was one of my favorite activities as a child. Now I love to watch my son make up songs and dance around. When you've got kids who want to make music, try this.

Just take

Empty film canisters
Rice
Paintbrushes
Masking tape (colored tape is fun)

Partially fill an empty film canister (camera stores are a great source) with rice. Use tape or glue to securely attach the top to the canister. Tape the filled canister to the top of the paintbrush. Just like that, a musical instrument is born.

Encourage older kids to create their own instruments out of household items.

Shift the Sand Inside

Haul it in! Shovel it in! I know it sounds crazy, but it's fun! Bring in a pile of sand. Put it on a tarp, on a tiled area, or in a child's swimming pool. Add trucks, construction equipment, and blocks. Children know how to do the rest! They will quickly become part of a construction crew working in the sand pile.

This is a great activity for those days when the weather just won't cooperate outside. Wouldn't children love to put on their shorts and play in the sandbox in the middle of winter? Fun, fun, real fun!

Just take

Sand
Tarp, tiled area, or small swimming pool
Toys for the sand
Construction crew

I shifted modes when...

_____

_____

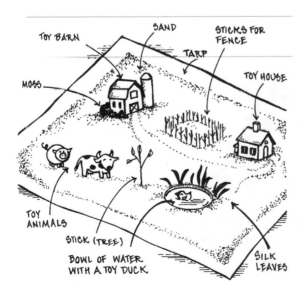

TOY BARN   SAND   STICKS FOR FENCE
TARP
MOSS
TOY HOUSE
TOY ANIMALS
STICK (TREE)
BOWL OF WATER WITH A TOY DUCK
SILK LEAVES

Shop 'Til You Drop

Save those shopping bags and used gift bags. The bags with handles are especially fun! Place the bags in different areas and see how many ideas children come up with. Children will sort, store, and carry all kinds of things. They might even hide something in their bag.

Just take

Shopping and gift bags

Little ones love to carry "stuff" around. You can offer them purses with handles and plastic carriers with handles.

What creative uses did children discover for the bags?

_____

_____

_____

_____

Smelly, Smelly

Do you surround children with pleasant smells or not-so-pleasant smells? Does your environment smell more like diapers, or does it smell of disinfectant and remind you of a pediatrician's office? Please the noses around you with pleasant smells by heating cinnamon sticks in a pan of water or baking bread in a machine or by hand. Bread not only smells good, it tastes great too.

The successful child is not the child that can memorize facts, but rather, the child that can ask the winnowing question. —*Jane Healy*

Just take

Smelly places
Smelly remedies
(bread machine, cinnamon sticks, cookies baking, etc.)

It smelled when...

_____

_____

_____

_____

Splatter Paint

(This was one of Carole's favorite things to do when she was four.)

Collect objects from nature (or any washable item or toy) and place them on top of a piece of paper. Place the screen over the object. Use a stiff-bristled brush (like a toothbrush) to rub paint over the screen. A really cool design will appear on the paper.

Just take

Objects from nature

Paper

Splatter screen (see construction directions below)

Toothbrush

Paint, slightly diluted to the consistency of liquid shoe polish

How to build your very own splatter screen:

Purchase a frame (or use an old frame) from a frame shop that is one-inch deep. Cut a piece of screening slightly larger than the outside dimensions of the frame. Use a staple gun (adult only) to securely attach the screen to the frame. Cover the sharp ends of the screening with duct tape.

Find something you are passionate about and keep tremendously interested in it.   —Julia Child

I will never make anything again because...

_____

_____

_____

_____

Squirt It On

Mix water and tempera paint (liquid or powder) in several squirt bottles (spray pumps work great, too). You should have several colors for the children to choose from. Place a large piece of paper on the easel and let the children squirt their way to beautiful art. For a different experience, hang a large sheet on the fence outside and let children squirt away. This colorful sheet will make a great backdrop for a play area.

Younger kids can have fun squirting with squirt bottles and water. You might want to let them squirt outside on windows and walls. When the weather is warm use large spray bottles. Cool off the kids as they play in the sun (swimsuits are the attire for this day).

Just take

Squirt bottles or spray pumps
Tempera paint
Water
Easel or painting surface
Paper or sheet

Never give up on a child. —Patricia Willis

We experienced _____ during this activity.

Squishy Squeezy

Begin with a bag that really seals tightly. Now add shaving cream (any brand). Squeeze it, squish it, and change the color by adding tempera paint. Enjoy!

Look in the bathroom for other items to feel in those bags. Try shampoo, bubble bath, or even bath salts. (I am feeling cleaner just thinking about this activity.)

Just take

Plastic bags that zip closed
Shaving cream
Tempera paint

This is a low maintenance idea, unless you forget to seal the bag!

Babies are such a nice way to start people.
—Don Herold

The most creative thing we added to a bag was...

Stains to Shout About

Relax, these stains are not on your clothes. These stains are made on paper using colored tissue scraps. Wet scraps of tissue paper. Children drag, place, or dump the wet tissue on a piece of paper. When you lift the soggy tissue paper, a colored stain is left behind. Children will shout with joy as they discover a whole new way to "paint" without paint.

Adults will shout at how easy it is to clean up after this activity.

Just take

Colored tissue paper
Paper
Water
Shouting kids and
adults (just kidding)

I shouted when...

Stick With Color

There is a whole palette of different tapes in a variety of colors. And, oh, the uses! Children will tape on the walls, on paper, on their clothes, on toys, on each other, on the floor. I think you get the point. They love to tape, and color only makes it better! (Be clear where it is NOT okay to tape.)

Just take

Tape
More tape
Variety of surfaces
that are okay
for taping

Bigger kids can use the tape to make roads and patterns on the floor or rug. For example, they can use tape to outline a basketball court or a hop-scotch game.

You got stuck when...

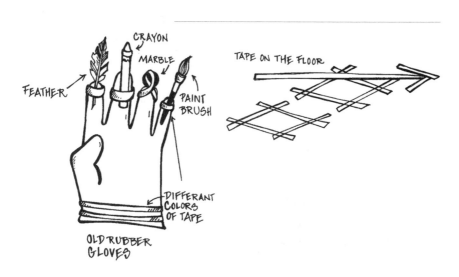

CRAYON
MARBLE
FEATHER
PAINT BRUSH
TAPE ON THE FLOOR
DIFFERANT COLORS OF TAPE
OLD RUBBER GLOVES

Stickers for Everyone

Kids love stickers! They are great for art, dramatic play, science, math (for patterns), and definitely near the mirror to be applied directly to children. Yes, they might decorate the mirror and the room with these stickers.

Put out stickers with various colors of construction paper, markers, glue, and scissors and encourage children to create pictures with the various materials.

> *Promising goodies to children for good behavior can never produce anything more than temporary obedience.* —*Alfie Kohn*

Just take

Stickers

Construction paper

Markers

Glue

Scissors

What will you "stick" to?

_____

_____

_____

_____

Sticky Steppin'

Pull out that contact paper, but not for laminating. It is time to get steppin' on that sticky stuff. Tape the contact paper on the floor, sticky side up. Let children walk across the contact paper (with shoes on or off). They get such a kick out of sticking to the paper. It is also fun to watch children discover that the paper is not sticky forever.

Just take

Contact paper
Masking tape

Big kids can predict in the morning if there will be any changes to the contact paper. Provide the children with various objects like leaves and sand and test out the sticking power of contact paper.

Every day's a kick!   —*Oprah Winfrey (A fellow Mississippian)*

I learned the following from children doing this activity:

_____

_____

_____

_____

String Them Along

Let children dip the string in globs of paint and swish them over the paper. Different colors make pictures with lots of variety. Different types of string will paint different lines. Once they have finished painting with the string, the strings can be pasted on another piece of paper for an entirely different kind of string art.

Bigger kids can dip the string in glue or thick sugar water and paste the string on a balloon. Once the string has dried the kids can pop the balloon. Great fun!

Children are the connoisseurs. What's precious to them has no price—only value.
    —Bel Kaufman

Just take

Short lengths of string or yarn
Tempera paint
Paper
Glue

Who liked this idea and why?

Take It Apart

What is it about children and their urge to take things apart? Why not help children channel this urge in appropriate ways. Save broken household items, such as phones, radios, bicycles: anything take would be fun to take apart. Offer space for children to have a Repair Shop for "repairing" these items.

Just take...

Broken stuff
Kid-size tools

Provide real tools for children to work with. Make sure the items are safe for children to play with, even if they are broken.

Bigger kids really get into this idea. If the big kids are having fun "repairing," take them to visit a real repair shop.

SKATE

Who do you predict will actually work in a repair shop when they grow up?

WATCH

SCOOTER

TOOLS

WALKIE-TALKIE

Take Out the Crayons

Next time you head outside for a walk, bring along the crayons and paper. Take a break in a shady spot and show children how to make crayon rubbings of objects in the great outdoors. Be sure and bring plenty of paper and different color crayons because the children will not want to stop with just one creation.

Toddlers may want to collect loose objects and bring them in to do crayon rubbings. It is also fun to paint directly on the collected objects.

Just take

Crayons
Paper
Objects from nature

Big kids can identify the objects they have captured in their rubbings using reference books and can create a book of nature treasures.

> *[Teaching] geared to the needs of learners requires...an enormous amount of flexibility, a tolerance for unpredictability, and a willingness to give up absolute control.* —Anonymous

This idea was fun because...

_____

_____

_____

_____

Tearing for Tantrums

If a child should throw a tantrum, here is a unique way to vent that anger or frustration. Let the child tear away their frustrations or fury by ripping the pages of an old telephone book. Tearing paper is a pre-cutting skill and a terrific way to vent intense feelings. When the child is finished tearing, he or she may be ready to talk about the feelings. This is a good time to ask.

Just take

Old telephone book
A tantrum
Private space for tearing

(This works for grownups, too.)

The shortest tantrum was...
The longest tantrum was...
The most interesting tantrum was...

Tell Me Your Story

Kids love to talk. You can record a child's conversations on paper or you can set up a tape recorder, complete with microphone. Allow children to tape their own voices. They can tell a story, sing a song, or just talk, talk, talk. A copy of this tape would make a great present.

Bigger kids may enjoy making their own book on tape. Encourage children to listen to a studio-recorded book on tape and then plan how they would like to create their own books. Encourage bigger kids to create sound effects by adding "action" noises or music to their book on tape.

Just take

Tape recorder with microphone and blank tapes, or paper and pencil

But don't stop there. Adults can get in on the action too. Record your child's favorite story. Then they can hear you read it, even when you are away or unable to sit down and read it with them. This is a super tape to add to your child's listening station at school.

The best story I heard was...

_____

_____

_____

_____

Textures to Touch

Give children a piece of clear contact paper. Peel off the backing, leaving the sticky side up. Provide a variety of collage items (buttons, feathers, confetti, sequins, colored tissue paper, etc.). The children place them on the sticky surface. Fold the contact paper over to seal this beautiful collection of treasures. This is fun to look at and to touch!

Just take

Clear contact paper
Collage items

If you are going on a walk give each child a bag to collect nature treasures for a different kind of collage. The textures of nature will be interesting to look at. Be sure to listen as the children tell you all about their treasures.

I touch the future. I teach! (I mold and create too.) —Avisia Whiteman

Parents are teachers too! —Kathy and Carole

I was touched when...

_____

_____

_____

....

The Art That Keeps Going and Going

Just when you think nothing can last a whole day, give this one a try. Tape a large piece of butcher paper on the wall or the floor. Put a bucket of crayons beside the paper and let children draw and color whenever they want throughout the day. No special display or assembly required. This art may last more than a day. It may last a week, a month, even a year. Okay, maybe not a year.

Next time you try this, put out markers or colored pencils. Just a little variety makes it seem like a whole new idea.

Just take

Butcher paper or a large sheet of chart paper
Crayons

How I kept this idea going:

_____

_____

_____

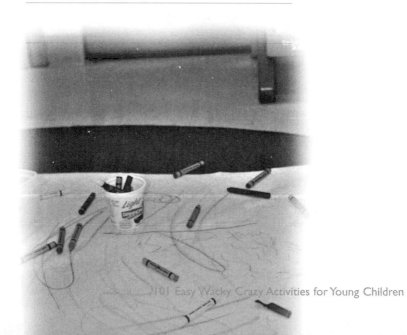

The Jar

Children tear the ever-popular colored tissue paper into small pieces (about 1" X 4"). Dip the pieces in glue and spread it across the outside of a jar. Layer the tissue paper on the jar, covering the entire jar for a beautiful creation. After the glue has dried, shellac the jar to preserve its beauty. This creates a one-of-a-kind jar!

Just take

Tissue paper
White glue
Jars (plastic bottles will work)
Shellac and paintbrush (only by adults in a well-ventilated area)

Use other kinds of paper on the jar. Try using cartoons from the newspaper or magazine pages that have a theme. This makes a great present for the adults in a young child's life.

This activity "jarred" me because...

TISSUE OR NEWSPAPER

JAR

TORN PAPER

GLUE

The Key Idea

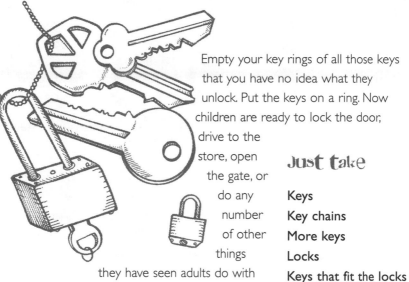

Empty your key rings of all those keys that you have no idea what they unlock. Put the keys on a ring. Now children are ready to lock the door, drive to the store, open the gate, or do any number of other things they have seen adults do with keys. Not only are keys for "locking" and "unlocking," they are shiny and make a great jingle-jangle in pockets. This is the perfect object for fun!

Just take

Keys

Key chains

More keys

Locks

Keys that fit the locks

Another key idea: Mix up locks and keys and encourage children to find the matching set. This will keep them busy for some time.

Children got keyed up when...

The Stocking Drop

Fill the toes of the old stockings with sand. Knot the open end. Dip the sand-filled stockings in tempera paint. Now drop the stockings on large butcher paper. Use a variety of colors for a lively look. Older children may want to see how changing the height from which the stocking is dropped changes the size of the image created on the paper.

Just take

Old stockings
Sand
Tempera paint
Butcher paper or other large paper

Just in case you're out of stockings and sand, here's another way to do this idea. Use a mesh netting bag (onions and citrus fruit are often packed in mesh netting bags) and fill it with a few marbles. Now you're ready to do the drop.

The great thing about The Stocking Drop is children can make the stocking painters themselves. This way of painting also uses large muscles instead of fine motor skills. This sometimes gets children to paint who might otherwise not be interested.

This idea just dropped out of the sky.

The Taste Test

How many of you eat persimmons? When was the last time you had a pomegranate or maybe a mango? It has probably been a while. There are so many different foods to taste. In some areas you might find an international market that carries all sorts of new foods. You might find that your grocer is willing to give you fruit at a discount if it has been on the shelf for a day or two. Join in on the tasting. You might discover something delicious. Hint: Be aware of any food allergies.

Just take

Unusual fruits and vegetables
Cutting board and sharp knife (adult only)

Another way to do a taste test is to invite families to come together and share foods they enjoy eating. This is great way to experience a variety of foods and have a grand food tasting. It is also a great way to bring families together.

We may misunderstand, but we do not misexperience. —Vine Deloria

More ideas tasteful enough for Emily Post are...

_____

_____

_____

_____

The Ultimate Party Hat

Start with plain colored party hats. Provide children with typical collage materials, such as, buttons, fabric strips, the ever-famous colored tissue paper, feathers, and anything else you have hanging around that you just won't throw away. Let children decorate the hats as they please. Every child has his or her very own, unique, one-of-a-kind party hat!

Just take

Plain colored party hats
Collage materials
Glue and tape

These are great for birthday parties. Of course there is really no need for a special occasion to celebrate. Have a "just because" celebration with hats, cake, and games. Everybody loves a party, so why save the fun for birthdays? Any day can be a party day.

I felt like celebrating when...

_____

_____

_____

SPARKLES

GLUE

STICKERS

PLAIN COLORED PARTY HATS

CONSTRUCTION PAPER

TISSUE PAPER

BUTTON

FEATHER

BUTTONS

This Paint Smells!

We're not talking about the time you left the paint in the pot too long. Yuck! Next time you put fresh paint in pots, add a little baby powder for a new and improved scent. But don't stop there. Try other good smells like vanilla or lemon extract. You might even explore spices. Painting is now more than just for the eyes.

As children explore these paints, talk with them about the smells and help them use words to describe the smells. This builds vocabulary for the future.

Older kids may like experimenting with scents and mixing their own smelly paint. You never know if there may be a future perfume creator in your presence.

Just take

Tempera paint
Baby powder
Spices or extracts
with strong smells
(optional)

Being a kid is dirty, messy, noisy work! —Carole Dibble

So, what do you think?

_____

_____

_____

_____

Tongue Painting

On a small paper plate, place a 1-tablespoon glob of corn syrup. Add a drop or two of food coloring. Now using tongues, lick your way to a masterpiece worthy of any refrigerator!

Just take

Small paper plates
Corn syrup
Food coloring

Don't be surprised if the younger ones lick their masterpiece all gone.

Children's reactions were....

_____

_____

_____

_____

Caution: *Tongue Painting* only works with corn syrup paint. Be sure children do not try it with tempera or watercolor paint. Also, be sure children do not try this "painting" technique to eat snacks or other foods.

Tracks

Little feet are s-o-o-o cute. Let those little feet create while they feel the squish-squash of paint between their toes. After they remove their shoes, let children step in the tempera paint and then walk across the butcher paper creating sweet footprints. This is a mural everyone is sure to appreciate. Cleanup is easy with a pan of warm, soapy water and towels.

This is another idea for making great gift wrap. (See idea #99.)

Just take

Butcher paper
Washable tempera paint
Feet
Dishpan of soapy water
Towels

I had to think quickly on my feet when...

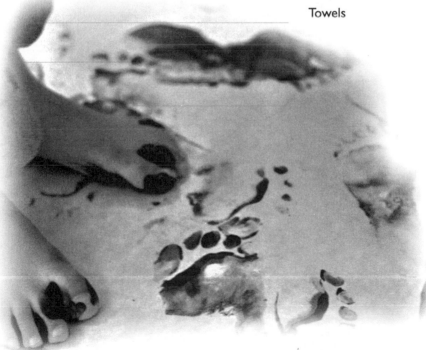

Unload the Laundry

You probably thought laundry baskets were for carrying clothes. Guess again! They have so many more uses, according to some boys we know (John Michael Lee and Patrick Dibble). Laundry baskets make great animal cages, space ships, boats, and much more. Any size basket will do—tall, short, even the old broken ones work. Just bring on the baskets.

Laundry baskets are fun for little ones to crawl into. Bigger kids will use the baskets as props for the elaborate stories they will develop.

Just take

Laundry baskets
Imagination

This was loads of fun because...

_____

_____

_____

_____

Wash It!

When you were a kid, did you think it was the greatest to help wash the car? What a way to complete a field trip or family outing! Let children wash the car or van. Provide buckets, a little soap, water, sponges, and some old towels for drying. Watch out, the kids might want to start their own business.

The little ones can have just as much fun washing play cars and trikes (and probably each other).

Just take

Buckets
Water
A water hose, if possible
Mild detergent (dishwashing detergent works well)
Sponges
Washcloths
Old towels

I knew this was a "wash" when...

_____

_____

_____

_____

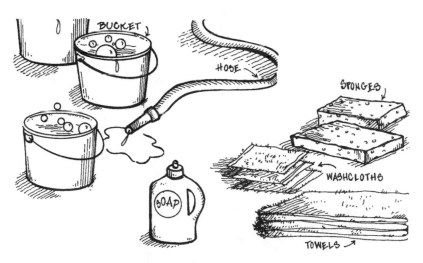

Water Spectrums

Have you ever been frustrated with the stains from food coloring that some-times linger after an art process? Here's a simple solution that costs only pen-nies to make! Add a couple of teaspoons of liquid tempera to a bottle. Next, add water. Continue to add paint until you have the color you want. It's safe! It's washable! It's affordable! (But NOT for use in food!) Another art crisis solved!

Just take

Water
Liquid tempera paint
Unbreakable bottles

Brain research shows children learn through dis-covery. Encourage children to discover new colors by offering cups of paint-colored water in the full spectrum, eyedroppers, and a plastic egg carton for mixing. How long do you think it will take before they discover gray?

Educating children begins with educating the grownups in their lives.
—Kathy H. Lee

I was mixed up when...

_____

_____

_____

_____

What's in a Box?

Provide children with a box (a big box, a little box, a rectangle box, a square box, any box). Children can begin by personalizing a box with paint. After the paint dries, the process continues with gluing, stamping, taping, cutting, pasting, drawing, and whatever else children desire.

The great thing about this box project is you don't know what each child will do with his or her box. The box may become a place where treasures are hidden. The box might become a space ship for exciting intergalactic travel. The box might hold a collection of very special things, or be a very special meeting place for friends. It's hard to tell just what incredible things might happen to this simple box.

BEWARE: This box may come to life.

Just take

A box

Paint

Paintbrushes

Paper

Glue

Stamps and inkpad

Stickers

More paint

I wasn't "square" when I did this activity because...

Without Form, But Not Without Purpose

Give children sponges to paint with that have no special shape. Allow them to dip the sponges in globs of tempera paint and sponge the paint onto paper. The purpose is not to learn shapes or colors or to print the shape that is part of the theme of the week. The purpose is for children to experiment with color and texture and to create a truly original work of art.

Just take

Pieces of sponge
Tempera paint
Paper

For older kids try the really flat sponges that they can cut into any shape. Wet these flat sponges so they expand to a normal sponge thickness. Now they're ready for painting. Kids will love making their own creations with sponges they designed.

Like snowflakes, no two children are alike.   —*Theresa Walker*

When I do this again, I will...

_____

_____

_____

_____

Wrap It Up

This idea is super, inexpensive, and usable. Cut butcher paper or brown wrapping paper into various sizes. Encourage children to paint on the paper using handprints or gadgets. Roll the paper up and tie a ribbon around it (after it has dried). Wrapping presents with this paper will make the gift even more valuable.

This project works great with all ages. Younger kids can use markers or stamps to make great wrapping paper and bigger kids can use tissue paper, paper bags, or newspaper and a variety of art media. Customized wrapping paper, what a great way for bigger kids to make spending money!

Just take

Butcher paper or brown wrapping paper
Scissors
Tempera paint, stamps, gadgets
Ribbon (personally, I love raffia)

We wrapped up this project when...

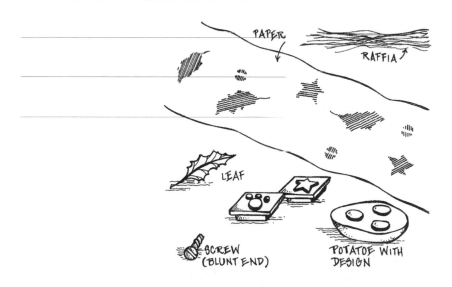

You Can Dance

That's right! Put on the music and dance. It's great for the body and the soul. Party stores have great dance tunes or pull out your favorites from high school. Whatever the beat, the kids will join in.

Just take

Tapes or CD's of music

A player

Play a dancing game. When you stop the music, everyone freezes. When the music starts again, so does the dancing. It helps younger kids to say "stop" and "dance" as the music stops and starts. Be sure to put on your dancing shoes on and dance along.

Take time to laugh—it is the music of the soul. —Anonymous

I felt like dancing when...

Just Imagine

This is the best idea in the book: Don't limit yourself to the ideas in this book. Come up with your own ideas. Go back to your childhood. What did you enjoy? What was your favorite thing to play? With a little imagination, you can bring these experiences to the children in your life!

Imagination is only intelligence having fun.
—George Sciabble

Just take...

Your imagination

If only you could have been there when...

_____

_____

_____

_____

Index

Recommended Title

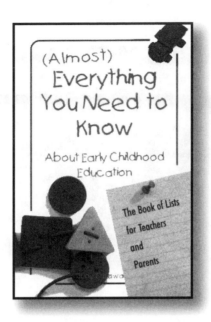

(Almost) Everything You Need to Know About Early Childhood Education

The Book of Lists for Teachers and Parents

Judy Fujawa

Veteran teacher Judy Fujawa offers over two decades of experience in her warm, witty book of lists. From the practical to the philosophic to the hilarious, these lists cover nearly everything one needs to know to work with and raise young children. 128 pages. 1998.

"Whether it's fun things to put in the water table or how to prepare children for kindergarten or things to do with boxes, you can always rely on *(Almost) Everything You Need to Know About Early Childhood Education* for useful, creative, effective ideas." —*Wisconsin Bookwatch*

ISBN 0-87659-192-6 / Gryphon House / 18275 / PB

Available at your favorite bookstore, school supply store or
order from Gryphon House

Making Make-Believe

Fun Props, Costumes and Creative Play Ideas

MaryAnn F. Kohl

Explore the world of make-believe with fun and easy-to-make props and costumes. Create a lifesize igloo out of milk jugs or put on a puppet show in your very own Lighted Box Stage! **Making Make-Believe** offers storybook play, games, cooking, mini-plays, dress-up costumes, puppet ideas, and more, to enrich children's play. Unlock the imaginations of young children, allowing them to create their own dramatic play experiences. With over 125 activities and projects, this book is packed with ideas for hours of creative fun! 192 pages. 1999.

ISBN 0-87659-198-5 / Gryphon House / 19674 / PB

Available at your favorite bookstore, school supply store or order from Gryphon House

300 Three Minute Games

Quick and Easy Activities for 2 to 5 Year Olds

Jackie Silberg

Use these short creative activities to delight and teach children whenever you need to fill an extra few minutes, or anytime just for fun. There are story games to build language skills, exercise games, quiet games, waiting games, stuck inside games, and more! Quick, simple games guaranteed to prevent bored children. 192 pages. 1997.

"No parent, teacher, or child-care center worker can afford to be without their own personal copy of **300 Three Minute Games!**" —*Children's Bookwatch*

ISBN 0-87659-182-9 / Gryphon House / 18657 / PB

Available at your favorite bookstore, school supply store or order from Gryphon House

The Big Messy* Art Book
*But Easy To Clean Up!

MaryAnn F. Kohl

Combine the joy of creativity, the delight of imagination, and the thrill of an art adventure. **The Big Messy Art Book** opens the door for children to explore art on a grander, more expressive scale. Paint a one-of-a-kind masterpiece from a swing, or try painting a hanging ball while it moves! With **The Big Messy Art Book**, you are giving children the opportunity to go beyond the ordinary and into the amazing! 144 pages. 2000.

ISBN 0-87659-206-X / Gryphon House / 14925 / PB

Available at your favorite bookstore, school supply store or order from Gryphon House

Preschool Art

It's the Process, Not the Product

MaryAnn F. Kohl

Anyone working with preschoolers and early primary age children will want this book. Over 200 activities encourage children to explore and understand their world through art experiences that emphasize the process of art, not the product. The first chapter introduces basic art activities appropriate for all children, while the subsequent chapters, which build on the basic activities in the first chapter, are divided by seasons. Activities are included for painting, drawing, collage, sculpture, and construction. Indexes organized by art medium and project name help teachers plan. 260 pages. 1994.

"...***Preschool Art*** is an essential addition to preschool, day care center, and kindergarten reference shelves..." —*Wisconsin Bookwatch*

ISBN 0-87659-168-3 / Gryphon House / 16985 / PB

Available at your favorite bookstore, school supply store or
order from Gryphon House

Recommended Title

Start Smart!

Building Brain Power in the Early Years

Pam Schiller

Did you know that emotions boost our memory? Or that small muscle exercises help the brain develop? Early experiences contribute to the future capacity of the brain. **Start Smart!** offers simple, straightforward ways to boost brain power with active exploration, repetition, sensory exploration, meaningful context, trial and error, and direct experience. All the activities are accompanied by explanations of how and why they help the brain develop. Easy and fun, **Start Smart!** will start young children ages three to six on their way to a future rich with learning! 192 pages. 1999.

ISBN 0-87659-201-9 / Gryphon House / 19378 / PB

Available at your favorite bookstore, school supply store or
order from Gryphon House

Recommended Title

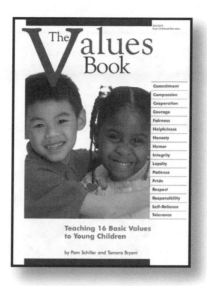

The Values Book

Teaching Sixteen Basic Values to Young Children

Pam Schiller and Tamera Bryant

Young children learn best by doing, and that includes learning values. **The Values Book** is packed with easy activities, projects, and ideas to help children learn values and build character, both individually and in groups. Each chapter addresses one of 16 different values, including understanding, patience, and tolerance. After defining the value, each chapter begins with questions to help adults clarify what that value means to them. The perfect book to introduce and strengthen the teaching of values in any early childhood classroom or home. 168 pages. 1998.

"**The Values Book** is a blueprint for teaching 16 basic, but very important values to children.... The suggested questions and activities are insightful, timely, and very creative.... It outlines how to consciously bring values back into our lives—values that each of us want for our children and the next generation."
—ForeWord Magazine.

ISBN 0-87659-189-6 / Gryphon House / 15279 / PB

Available at your favorite bookstore, school supply store or order from Gryphon House

Recommended Title

Tell It Again!

Easy-to-Tell Stories with Activities for Young Children

Shirley C. Raines and Rebecca Isbell

The authors of ***Tell It Again!*** have compiled the best tips and tricks of expert storytellers and teachers in a single book. Through retellings of 18 well-loved children's stories, teachers and parents can capture the attention and imagination of young children. It's easy to use: just read the story, noting the hints and tips (when to raise your voice or make a funny face). Then put the book away, pick up the accompanying outline with important story points, and spin your tale! Extend the story with dozens of activities specially created to fit each story. 192 pages. 1999.

ISBN 0-87659-200-0 / Gryphon House / 19628 / PB

Available at your favorite bookstore, school supply store or
order from Gryphon House

Recommended Title

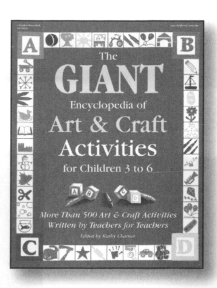

The **GIANT** Encyclopedia of Art and Craft Activities for Children 3 to 6

Edited by Kathy Charner

Teacher created, classroom-tested art activities to actively engage children's imaginations! The result of a nationwide competition, these art and craft activities are the best of the best. Just the thing to add pizazz to your day! 568 pages. 2000.

The GIANT Encyclopedia of Art and Craft Activities joins our best-selling GIANT Encyclopedia series which includes *The GIANT Encyclopedia of Circle Time and Group Activities*, *The GIANT Encyclopedia of Theme Activities*, and *The GIANT Encyclopedia of Science Activities*.

ISBN 0-87659-209-4 / Gryphon House / 16854 / PB

Available at your favorite bookstore, school supply store or order from Gryphon House